Dressing up
and other stories

Dressing up page 3

Tom the dragon page 11

The elves and the shoemaker
page 23

Nelson

Dressing up

"Mum, Mum, I am going to be
in a play at school.
Can I have your best hat for
the play?" said Anna.
"Oh dear, not my best hat," said Mum.

"But I must take something," said Anna.
"Can I have your new dress?"
"No, you can't," said Mum.
"It is too big for you and
I want to wear it," said Mum.

"Well, can I have your
new red coat?" said Anna.
"Don't be silly," said her Mum.
"I will think of something you can take."

Anna cried and cried.
"I want a hat, or a dress,
or a red coat," she said.
Mum was cross.
"You are very silly," said Mum.
"I have told you, Anna.
You can't have my hat, or dress, or coat.
Now it is bedtime."

The next morning Anna ran down to breakfast.
"Have you got something for me, Mum?" said Anna.
"Yes," said Mum.
"It is in this box.
You can open it at school."

Anna went to school.
She took the box with her.
It was too small to have
the red coat in it.
It was too small to have
a dress in it.
It was too big to have
a hat in it.

"Hello, children," said Miss Jones.
"Have you got something to wear
in the play?"
"I have got my Dad's hat," said Peter.
"I have got my Gran's dress," said Emma.
"I have got my Mum's
old coat," said Bill.

"That is good," said Miss Jones.
"What have you brought, Anna?"
"I don't know," said Anna.
"My Mum gave me this box."
She gave the box to Miss Jones.
Miss Jones took off the lid.
The children all wanted to see.

"Look," said Miss Jones.
"It is a pair of silver shoes."
"Ooooh," said the children.

"We can act a very good play now.
We will act Cinderella and
the silver slipper," said Miss Jones.
"And you can be Cinderella, Anna."
Then all the children clapped and
Anna was very happy.

Tom the dragon

Tom the dragon was sad.
All the other dragons
could make smoke and fire.
But not Tom.
No smoke and fire came from his nose.
"I want to be like all the other dragons,"
he said and he began to cry.

"Don't cry," said his mother.
"Don't be sad.
You are still small.
Eat a lot, play a lot.
You will get big.
Then you will make smoke and fire
like the other dragons."

Tom ate a lot and played a lot.
But still he could not make smoke and fire.
One year passed.
Still Tom could not make smoke and fire.

The other dragons began
to laugh at Tom.
"You can't make smoke and fire
like us," they said.
"We won't play with you.
You are not brave, like us."
Tom was big, but he still
could not make smoke and fire.
He did not cry but he was very sad.

"Don't be sad," said his mother.
"It will happen in time."
But Tom did not want to wait.
He wanted to make smoke and fire now.
He wanted to show the other dragons
that he was brave.

"I will run away," said Tom.
"I will go to the old wizard
on top of the big hill.
Perhaps he will help me."

When it was dark, Tom ran away.
The wizard lived very, very far away.
Tom walked all alone.

At last he came to the foot of the hill where the wizard lived.
He went to the very top.
There was the wizard's cave.

Tom told him his story.
"I am very old now," said the wizard.
"I hope my magic still works.
You are a brave dragon to have come
all this way by yourself.
I would like to help you.
I will try."

The wizard had a big pot.
He began to put things in it.
He put in all sorts of things:
 leaves and rats' tails,
 wool from sheep,
 a dog's bark, stars and other things.
He began to stir the pot.
He made a spell.

Green smoke began to fill the cave.
There was a bang, then a flash of fire.
"Try and make smoke now,"
the wizard said.
Tom tried.
But no smoke or fire came.
Smoke still came from the pot.
The wizard and Tom went out of the cave.
"I am so sorry," said the wizard.
"My magic doesn't seem to work."

"I am so sad," the wizard said.
He looked as if he would cry.
"I don't mind any more," Tom said.
"I don't need smoke or fire.
I know I am brave."
Just then there was a flash of fire and lots of smoke.
"It is coming from me," Tom shouted.
"Your magic did work."

"Yes," the old wizard said.
"It did work.
It just took time.
I am so happy," the wizard said.
"So am I," Tom said.
They gave each other a hug and said goodbye.

Then Tom set off for home.
He walked all alone.
But now he was happy.
Soon he would be home.
Then he would show
all the other dragons that he too
could make smoke and fire.

The elves and the shoemaker

The shoemaker and his wife were sad.
They had no food and they had no money.
They had only one bit of leather left.
"I can make one more pair of shoes
tomorrow," said the shoemaker.
"But how shall we live after that?"
He carefully cut out the last pair of shoes.
Then he and his wife went upstairs to bed.

In the morning the shoemaker and his wife came downstairs.
They saw a pair of shoes on the table.
"Who made the shoes?" asked his wife.
"And who finished them?" asked the shoemaker.
They did not know.
But they were very happy.
The door bell rang and a lady came into the shop.

"I want a pair of shoes," she said.
"I like that pair."
She gave the shoemaker
five silver pieces.
"Now I can buy some more leather,"
said the shoemaker.
"I can make some more shoes.
And we shall get some food."
He went out and bought some leather.
Before he went to bed
he sat down at his table.
He carefully cut out two pairs of shoes.
Then he and his wife went upstairs to bed.

In the morning the shoemaker and
his wife came downstairs.
They saw two pairs of shoes on the table.
"Who made the shoes?" asked his wife.
"And who finished them?"
asked the shoemaker.
They did not know.
But they were very happy.
The door bell rang and a family
came into the shop.
"We need some shoes," they said.
They gave the shoemaker
twenty silver pieces.

"Now I can buy some more leather,"
said the shoemaker.
"I can make some more shoes.
And we shall get some food."
He took his donkey and
went into the street.
He bought lots of leather.
Before he went to bed
he sat down at his table.
He carefully cut out eight pairs of shoes.
Then he and his wife went upstairs to bed.

But they did not go to sleep.
They hid behind the curtain
at the top of the stairs.
They wanted to know who
was helping them with their work.
Suddenly the front door opened.
They saw two little men.
They were very thin and
their clothes were old.
But they looked happy.
The little men sat down at the table and
began to work.

Next day the shoemaker and his wife
were very busy.
The shop was full of people and
they sold lots of shoes.
The shoemaker and his wife wanted to say
thank you to the two little men.
They made them some tiny clothes.
They made two tiny pairs of trousers,
two tiny shirts,
two tiny jackets and two tiny hats.
And they made two tiny pairs of boots.

Before they went to bed the shoemaker
and his wife put all the new clothes
on the table.
Then they went upstairs to bed.
But they did not go to sleep.
They hid behind the curtain
at the top of the stairs.
Suddenly the front door opened.
They saw the two little men.

The little men ran to the table and when they saw the tiny new clothes they began to smile.
They put on the trousers and the shirts.
They put on the jackets and the hats.
And they each put on a pair of boots.
They began to dance and sing.
They danced to the front door.
They danced out of the house and they danced away down the street.

The shoemaker never saw
the little men again.
But he and his wife will never forget
how the two little men helped them
when they were poor and hungry.
And they will never forget how they sang
and danced out of the house and
away down the street.